My Mother's Medicine

poems

Maxine Susman

GRAYSON BOOKS
West Hartford, CT
www.GraysonBooks.com

Published by Grayson Books
West Hartford, Connecticut

Interior book and cover design by Cindy Stewart

Photos courtesy of Coleen Marks and Maxine Susman
WMCP Class of 1937 picnic photo courtesy of Legacy Center Archives,
Drexel University College of Medicine, Philadelphia.

For my sister Rita and brother Bill

and in loving memory of our parents,
Florence Carol Levin, M.D. and Benjamin R. Susman, M.D.

Together we are glad, you whose daughters are reaching after four years of hard work, a much desired goal; with their teachers, who have set before them both the difficult task and the intellectual feast...the art and science of healing...the happy day when you will look proudly upon the shingle that lures patients to your office.

All that has been learned about the maintenance of health and vigor...the prevention and cure of disease is of little avail unless it is interpreted to the people and placed within their reach....Enter upon your profession's work with an eager sense of adventure.

Dean Martha Tracy, *Commencement Address to the Graduating Class of the Woman's Medical College of Pennsylvania, 1937*

Contents

My Mother Steps into Women's History

My mother attended the Woman's Medical College of Pennsylvania from 1933-37, during the Great Depression and the rise of Nazi Germany. Woman's Med, founded in 1850, was the first women's medical school in the world, and the last one to survive in the United States. It was a leader in women's health care, obstetrics and gynecology, pediatrics, public health, and the emerging field of preventive medicine; the only medical school administered by women, with a woman president and a majority of women on the Board of Trustees. Most important, the College hired women professors in all fields of medicine, who served as teachers, role models, and mentors.

By the late 1960s, when women finally began to enter medical schools in growing numbers, Woman's Med decided to admit men in order to stay afloat. It continued to evolve, and was absorbed eventually into the Drexel University College of Medicine.

Back in my mother's time, Woman's Med outlasted a vote in 1935 by the male medical establishment to revoke accreditation, largely—if implicitly—due to bias against women in the profession. Woman's Med faced the threat, raised the funds, made improvements, and endured. From 1920 to 1968 it graduated between twenty and fifty new doctors a year—small numbers from a small school, but representing fully a fifth to a third of all women medical graduates.

My mother was one of them. Her personal story, as a Jewish girl from Brooklyn, daughter of a Russian immigrant, first in her family to graduate from college, becomes part of the history of women in medicine.

Before

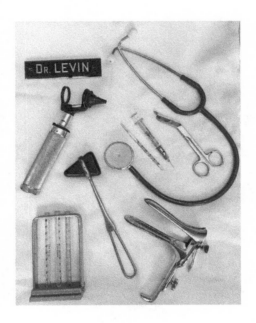

Certificate of Naturalization

Height: five feet two inches.
Color: white.
Complexion: dark.
No visible distinguishing marks.

Origin Russia, somewhere in Russia,
a big country spewing Jews.

Wife Bertha, 26 yrs, and three little ones:
Minnie, Herbert, and Florence, 1 yr. old.
Place of residence: 300 West 68th Street
in the City of New York,

on the 2d day of December year of our Lord
nineteen hundred and fifteen
(not his lord or his wife's or his children's but)
the lord of good English, of italics,
of his new world,

signed by   *Reuben Levin*
                    in the middle of the page,

Be it remembered that
be admitted as
entitled to be
a citizen of the United States of America.

Identity within a thin yet ornate border,
signed, sealed, embossed,

the O R I G I N A L copy folded in thirds
then in half, arriving in a legal envelope,
To be given to the person naturalized—

He unfolds the paper, smoothes it flat under glass,
gives it a metal backing and a sturdy frame.

He came in time.
Some years until the door slammed shut.

My mother was born in 1914,

the year World War I broke out in Europe,
a year before her father became a citizen,

two years before Margaret Sanger
opened the first birth control clinic
in America, right in Brooklyn,

four years before Spanish flu reached New York,
the Armistice was signed,
her baby brother was born.

Age six when women won the vote,
ten when the law changed to bar all Asians
and set quotas for Italians and Jews,

fifteen when the stock market crashed in '29
a year before she graduated high school,
eighteen when FDR became president

the year before she started med school
and her father died of pneumonia.

In '37 she graduated during the Depression,
the year before Kristallnacht—
two years later came the start of World War II,
last letter from relatives in Minsk.

Pearl Harbor, '41. She was living in Manhattan,
private practice, hospital job, Brooklyn Board of Health.
'44, the first time civilians received penicillin.
Next year the atom bomb ended the War.

She met my father still in uniform,
Royal Canadian Medical Corps,
they married in two months.

Her world and the larger world continue
decades more: husband, children, work,
joys, sorrows, success, dementia

until she dies a month before turning 96.
History doesn't end, but histories do—

right after/   \ right before
something changes everything.

For My Grandfather

If I imagine my grandfather
whom I never knew
but my mother stored in her heart,
if I invent him

which of course I can't.
Love a stranger?
I failed her in this, not knowing him
past remorse, not comprehending
her residue of grief.

Can't be his voice.
Impossible to speak for him,
to him, so close but missing—
only improvise words, remarks,

what he thought about things
he thought about, what struck him
as funny, the look on his face
any given moment,
his gait and timbre,

what he might have said to me.
No one alive now who knew him,
who carries him ahead.
A few traces—stories, tilt of the chin
I can pass along,

a picture or two, though the one
of him and my grandmother side by side,
the one on the windowsill
in my mother's room
in assisted living

which I remember putting in a box
when we had to clear out
all her belongings by the next day,
that picture disappeared.

Reuben's Voice

If a man can be a rebbe,
why can't a woman be a doctor?
Don't answer, I know, it's not
the same for them. Why not? Tell me.
A woman can be a doctor
just like a man can be a whole new person,
nu?
A boy in Russia, man in America,
same as I was, not the same.
A woman can be a doctor, why not?
I learned the ropes, married my Tillie,
built a business, raised four kids,
so why shouldn't our girl be a doctor?
Nu,
if you allow yourself to be possible
anything is possible. Sky's the limit.
Flossie, *Chai Feiga*, my little dark Flossie,
there's prejudice here too
but see where you can go.

For My Grandmother

I was a child, didn't think
who you'd once been in your own home
past the treasures you brought
when you came to live with us.
Photos, books, soup pot, candlesticks.
Any glimpse of you
a child, a girl, a mother?
I don't remember.
You're standing on the terrace,
polka dot silk, white gloves, handbag,
squinting into the sun.
Where are we going?

I'm sitting on your lap
before I could read, the two of us
reading to each other.
Later, you called me your walking stick,
we strolled the sidewalk
in front of the house,
you too frail to manage alone.
I loved you, that you needed me.

Tillie's Voice

At her age Reuben was fresh off the boat—she went off to college.
At that age, I was having babies—she's learning to deliver them.
I helped Reuben with his English, kept his accounts
while I kept house and raised the kids. Things worked out—
Brooklyn, a nice house, he brings home surprises—
phonograph, electric washer—he likes the latest
and I keep up with him, what's in the news.
Women earn their own money now, Jewish boys are doctors—
why not our Flossie, with those grades? She'll hold her own
among the men. Educated, listened to.
She asked me, growing up, *Mama, what do you think?*

No bed of roses, turned-up noses and turned-away faces,
but could it be a full life, good life, for her?
Not the happiness I wanted or thought she'd have,
not what anyone in the family has done before—
her professors tell them married to the work—
keep going, my *tochtele*. I want this for you.

Flossie

They think she's reading. She slips downstairs.
She's been called papoose, gypsy, even adopted.
Where'd you get those big black eyes?

Who am I, she thinks, what do I look like,
am I American?
Olive skin, even darker than Papa's—
Oh that's just Flossie, just our Floss.

Mama is fair, hazel eyes, auburn hair
she pins up in tortoise-shell combs.
The others have her skin, even the baby.

Mama and her friends play canasta,
sip glasses of tea, nibble rugelach.
They wear cameos pinned to good dresses,
lace hankies, watches on gold chains.

She goes back up to Mama's bureau—
powders her face with the big talcum puff,
then downstairs again to show off like them.

Always something, that one, white as a sheet!
How she gets into things—
Mama tries to make it better,
We're not laughing at you we're laughing with you

but Flossie's not laughing,
tears smear her perfect made-up cheeks,
she runs to her room where she can think—

too dark to be pretty so better be smart—
who she could be, who she really is.

The Log, James Madison High School, 1930

Character is what a man actually is. Reputation is different. Reputation is only what he is said to be. He may be better or worse than his reputation. He is never better nor worse than his character.

—From the Address to the Graduating Class

Either women are men, or they have no character.

Senior Advisors:
      large oval photo of a man encircled by head-shots of six women.

Administrative Heads:
      twelve men in vested suits.

Debating Team   Traffic Squad   First Aid Club   even Cheerleaders
      Boys. All boys.
Press Club: seven boys, one girl.
Mostly boys in Law Club and Go-Getters.
Yearbook Staff: ten boys, three girls.

Football, soccer, swimming, basketball, track, cross country, rifle.
      Boys.
No pictures of sports for girls,
      they pose for the Dolly Madison Club, the Drama Society.

Ad pages in the back:
      Three months after the Crash of '29
      business schools promise *Positions Guaranteed*,
Gitlitz's on Kings Highway, *Every Bite a Juicy Delight*.

The graduates:
      fifty-one pages, nine to a page, Abrams to Zivkin,
          the boys serious, not smiling,
          the girls half-smiling—

My mother is an L, half-way down,
            Booster Club, swimming (she never learned),
            hockey (did she?), skipping grades, off to NYU,
She's—oh well, just Floss,

bobbed hair, v-neck sweater, a full grin.

NYU Downtown

He said, *Do your best.*
He said, *Nothing wrong with being a girl. Or smart.*
Or Jewish. Sounding Jewish.

Which she worked on and she doesn't.

He said, *There's no reason not to.*
Go ahead, give it a try.
He said, *Go out with college boys*
but stay away from socialists.

She brought home a little blue pipe
from a smoke shop on Eighth Street.
The rage, all her friends had them.

He said, *Women smoke pipes now?*

Held out his palm. *Let me see.*
She gave it. He turned it over,
the stem snapped. He looked at her
and gave it back.

She said nothing, all of seventeen.

He said, *Don't get ahead of yourself.*
He said, *You can be anything you want.*

Treat

I'll treat
        coconut layer   butterscotch sundae
           new outfit   tickets to a show

treat me to one of your hugs why don't you

call for an appointment   come to the Office
        what's on your mind   where does it hurt
           behind closed doors

annual check-up
        no cause for alarm   clean bill of health   runs in the family

        an honest answer   professional courtesy

first do no harm   treat like one of your own   give as good as you get

a treat for sore eyes   kiss where it hurts

self-medicate   write your own scrip
        medicine chest   nail polish / aspirin / hair pins / Tums
        cold compress   pull the shades   kiss goodnight

can't keep her down   physician heal thyself
        fresh air and sunshine   three times a day   take a deep breath

be on the lookout   a new horizon
        pie in the sky

life's little pleasures   smile for the camera   surprise in the fridge

delayed gratification   cure for what ails you

        treat yourself   it's later than you think

           the best is yet to come

During

Matriculation Book, September 14, 1933

at the Archives of Women in Medicine, Philadelphia

She steps up when her turn comes
to the volume of gold-tooled leather.

Signs the wide double page.
Pressure of their pens, shades of ink
as each young woman writes herself in.

My mother spreads
        Florence C. Levin
                        across the blank field.

A bold hand, slight flourish
as if she has practiced claiming
the space of her row, ready
for things she's not ready for
until she finds them waiting,

and this is where I meet her signature,
catch my breath—a glimpse
of my nineteen-year-old mother
dated two days before my birthday
a lifetime before she thought of me.

The archivist points, a scribbled note
near her name: *Matriculation cancelled.*
Unexplained.
                When her father died?
Yet she graduated with the others.

Basement archives. Volumes, boxes, files.
Ignore, retrieve, re-shelve—
What did she feel,
scripting herself on the waiting page?
Each young woman signs in only once.

Pneumonia

Just weeks into the fall.
He has a bad cold,
no need to come home.

Come home.

He's coughing but smiling,
kibbitzing he already paid
her school bill, even hard times
people need plumbers
just like they do doctors,

she agrees to what he wants,
returns to school.
In a week he's dead.

Forty-seven years old.
A few years before penicillin.

She rushes back from Philly,
in her new coat sobbing on the train

to sit shiva with the family,
Mama, Minnie, Herbie, Jack,
the house overflowing
with condolences and food,

then strangely emptied.
She wants to stay home.
They need her at home,

don't they need her?
No, Mama says, holding her close,
go back to school.

After / Before

What her first month at med school
taught of life and death:

Love and prayer are not a cure.
A plot in Mt. Lebanon Cemetery
costs more than a year's tuition.

She changed that fall from Papa's Flossie,
Flossie the whiz kid, the dark girl from Brooklyn

to Florence who will graduate F. Carol Levin,
the name on her diploma, name on her shingle.

Carol, my father called her. Carol to friends.

Specialist in Diseases of the Lungs.

Yom Kippur in Histology Lab

May you have an easy fast,
the customary greeting, but instead of shul and shofar
she rushed off to the lab, taking her place
among young women who never skipped a class
as they might a meal.

Denying herself forgiveness
she davens head bent over her microscope,
peering down at a small glass plate
smeared with a drop of her own sputum—

what the cells confess and could atone for,
secrets she can swab from within herself,
the words of my mouth and meditations of my heart—

while back home she knows they're fasting,
nothing will pass their lips but words,
Alvenu Malchenu, Our Father, our King,
we have sinned before you,
prayers and melodies rising from dry throats
as the holy day wears on.

She leaves the lab at dusk, light-headed,
looks up to find the earliest star,
the one her father would watch for
as he left synagogue,
sign it's time to break the fast.

The Animal Shed

stood past the new College Hall. Walk by
at the right times, you hear them being fed.

She watched a truck unload a batch of strays,
barking, yelping, snapping, herded inside

to be hosed, kept in clean cages, treated
for eczema and worms. When they're needed

brought to the Path Lab, with its cabinets
of embryos and specimens in jars.

A large mutt sleeps on a table under ether.
The Greater Good, the Higher Good,

better a cat than a human, a dog than a child.
She can't be squeamish,

she's seen people sleeping on the streets in Philly,
knows round-ups are spreading through Germany

while she's safe, her world stays safe—
these creatures whose yowls ring in her ears,

different just because treated that way?
She notes the divide between who's petted

and who's sacrificed, between those caught
and those at large. Whom we treasure

and whom we briefly value.
Vivisection, surgery—she learns to doctor.

The animals teach her anesthesia,
a numbing so the necessary can proceed,

but why is this not wrong?

The Ambidextrous Professor

It looks something like this.
Drawing with both hands   lecturing on.

She listens less to his words   than his hands
          dance and hover   freestyle, separate

faint clicks   hiss of chalk
          his fingers form muscles   render bone

most eloquent when he turns his back
          concentrates on imaging

He warns the class away
from black-and-white clarity—

the moving tissue of his fingers and wrists
          play bass and treble—
          densities of color
                    feel   flex

left hand draws the left lung   right hand draws the right
I'd say a pretty fair rendering
          or   *I'll just go back and touch this up a bit.*

Both hands round their perfect circles
          fill in stipples or hatching
                    synchronize delicate webs of membrane

but he tosses off their admiration
          he assumes or pretends   they all could do it too

          this pas de deux—

sketch bodily constellations on the blackboard sky.
More than anatomy he teaches

                    Learn to draw with both hands,
                    don't waste your precious time.

Her Cadaver

Old woman.
She holds the scalpel
as she's been shown.

Runs out to vomit.
First cut. She must.
No feelings,
just for now.

Layer under layer
what they shared,
woman and woman,

predictable until
she reaches
the anomalies.

Autopsy, a lesson
in self: the body
as an object
you can open,

dissect into parts
and still not meet
the stranger,

the same as you
painting your nails,
brushing on mascara,

not probing
the truths inside
your waiting body.

She pulls the sheet
over her heart
to press ahead,
relieved to begin.

Winter Study

A list of rooms in the neighborhood of the College...approved by the Dean's Office and available as lodgings....Rates range from $3.00-$5.00 per week.
—86th Annual Announcement of the Woman's Medical College of Pennsylvania, 1935-36

It rained all day. The bus was late.
The class was long. The lab was hard,
she'll have to catch up

        Physiology, Bacteriology

she stops at the bake shop—cinnamon buns!
then hurries down the windswept street
with their fragrance in her book bag,

instead of Tennyson and Millay
Latin's the language to memorize now—
an evening of cramming body parts—

        Pharmacology, Surgical Principles

Professor likes to say
Nomenclature anticipates diagnosis
and potentially a cure.

She turns the key to her rented room,
flicks on the light, sheds wet things,
settles her textbooks, fills the kettle

        Public Hygiene and Sanitation, Pathology

like home, staying up late before exams.
She'll skip supper, make a pot of tea
to last the rainy cinnamon night.

Course in Physical Diagnosis, Second Year

You learn to touch strangers.
You watch it done then reach your hand
to imitate, feeling for the pulse
in your partner's wrist, her neck.
You learn what you find out
simply by bending a limb,
pressing an armpit or belly.
You'll hold the orb of a stethoscope
to the quadrants of someone's back
and underneath her breasts.
You'll get the feel of it, you're told.

Skin Graft

I don't ask for a pound of flesh,
says the professor, *Just a small patch*
of epidermis. So she volunteers.

The professor freezes her upper thigh,
slits it with a scalpel like a fruit knife—
then clamps and peels away an oval
inch of skin. She has to look

at what she doesn't feel.
Does not expect to flinch.

Professor freezes her inner arm,
flicks the scalpel like a feather,
quick incision then places the skin
from her thigh onto the open spot,

next works the curved blade
of the suture needle, a seamstress
who stitches a blank tattoo
and promises no mark,

but oh, not true,
it's hers to practice on,
here—
she'll keep it close—
her self-inflicted wound,
her voluntary scar.

Lighting Up

They found stylish ways to offer or accept,
head tilted, lips pursed like in the movies,
which fingers, a whiff, and tip the ash—

sexier than gum, and what's the harm?

People smoked on the street, the train,
in lobbies, parks, offices, restaurants, stores,
doctors' waiting rooms. Of course, in bed.

After dinner: a cordial, a cigarette.

They kept ashtrays in their rooms,
souvenirs of good times, trips,
maybe a favorite keepsake from home

while they learned to read x-rays,
spot a lesion on the lungs.

A car window rolls down an inch or two
like a stocking—
a cig flicked before the light turns.

Your first cigarette. Your first autopsy. Your first kiss.

Accreditation

Quotes are from *Minutes of the Association of American Medical Colleges* at their Annual Meeting, Toronto, October 1935.

A limited number of good men   gentlemen   chaps   men   fellows
           (For he's a jolly good)
preparing the medical men   men who make good students
    he   him   he   they   him

Report on the new aptitude test:
Does not predict whether a man   will have manual dexterity as a surgeon
his stamina   his family background
    It predicts only his chance of studying medicine

*

Miriam Butler M.D. and Catherine Arthur M.D. sit in the crowded hall
among men whose wives are off to shop and sight-see

politely received   doors held   gallantries
    (before the suited backs close ranks again)

Dr. Butler and Dr. Arthur stare ahead as the delegates vote
to place their College on probation
    —the only surviving medical school for women—

duly seconded and approved.

*

Final entry: the one mention of women,
a motion *to thank our Toronto hosts*
for their courtesies, accommodations, and good will.

    Our appreciation of the wonderful entertainment
    that has been given to the ladies.

President Starr Reacts

This is a man-equation; anti-feminists are in the saddle.
—Sarah Logan Wister Starr, from her cruise ship in Cape Town,
South Africa

Stuffed-shirt Old Boys. Self-serving reasons.
What really galls them, women run our school—
the labs, lecture halls, offices, committees—

clear as day, they want to keep the jobs
when times are tough. They dare complain
"About 40 percent of the students are Hebrews"
evidence we don't measure up.

Sure, whoever meets our yard-stick
and scrapes up her tuition has a shot—
gumption and drive, possibilities—

we turn them into damn good doctors,
I've come to envy girls like them.
No Logan woman works for pay—
Granddad's will spells that out flat—
we give ourselves to worthier causes,

well, I've got his head for business,
I simply have a gift of going out collecting money
and making people give it—

Chevalier Jackson will step into my shoes,
our figurehead male M.D., he'll appease
that crowd of hidebound sawbones

while I roll up my sleeves and get to work again.
People don't say no to me.

Nicodemus

He slides down the birth canal
over and over

black newborn doll
through the pink-and-white insides
of his cutaway model mother,

each time to a pair of waiting white hands.

Her turn. Everyone watching
her hands tremble a little
he tumbles out
thrilled she catches him
lifts him by the heels
slaps to make him come alive—

Nicodemus arrives
perfect, no complications,

but Professor asks what if
breech, stuck shoulder, cord around the neck?

That will come later in the term. For now
Nicodemus is taken back and put away.

No one in the class has a child yet,
years since they played with dolls

but soon they'll deliver real babies,
be given mothers of their own
on the ward, in the walk-ups,
newborns bawling in their hands.

Baby Clinic

At the Barton Dispensary

She's one of the young women in white coats
standing behind a scale at long enamel tables.

Mothers wait
a line out the door
soothing their babies bundled in shawls—

Who's next?
A mother unwraps her child
for a fledging doctor to examine,

a cloth laid on the cold steel basket,
the naked baby
dips the scale between them.

*

The room fills
with noise, bawl of baby cries
taken by surprise,
sucking of breast-seeking, mothers' coos,

admiring clucks, hers and the others
who press the aureoles of their stethoscopes

to tiny chicken-chests,
try to interpret a Babel of accents,
gestures, questioning faces,

this the rotation where she's meant to adopt
a kind authority,

learn to evade struggling little limbs,
slide the weights,

adjust arrow to notch
for a true reading,
then give back the infant to its mother.

She's starting to enjoy herself,
takes a deep breath between babies.

Suffrage

She's on the bus headed to the Clinic
where mothers with infants wait in line,
she thinks, I'm only one generation ahead of them,

she can see row on row of high school classmates
receiving diplomas, a sea of immigrant parents
behind them, citizens who pledge allegiance,
pay taxes, obey the laws,

and she remembers being small
perched high on her father's shoulders,
seeing Mama march with thousands of women
down the middle of Fifth Avenue,

banners with a million signatures—
her father throwing back his head laughing
What a country! Women! Jews!

How her parents in '32 walked arm-in-arm
to vote for Roosevelt. *The only thing to fear
is fear itself*—not true, look around,
bank lines, bread lines, Hoovervilles, clinic lines,

the other day she joined a group of women
around a Union table, LEARN TO VOTE
in English and Yiddish, *Register Here*—

what's it like inside the booth?
Private, she thinks, you draw the curtain
as for someone in labor giving birth—

It's her stop next, she has time and change
for a sandwich at the automat,
a week from now she'll stand in line to vote.

Finals

White count, red count, hemoglobin, urinalysis,
sound the chest, feel for the liver, read the x-ray.

Lab, library, curled in her chair in her room,
she gets up an hour early stays up an hour late

        shoulder rolls, stretches, shimmy to the radio

laughing with her friends at the Commons
she looks out at shade trees, the campus lawn,

knows that men sell pencils nearby in front of the Art Museum
and live in caves they've dug behind its walls,

knows the Hooverville in Central Park—a judge tore it down
but gave each man two bucks from his own pocket

        while she's safe and sound, studying,

knows in Germany Nazis burn books, beat up Jews—
their own Dr. Kuhlenbeck escaped in time

        two exams tomorrow, she must keep studying

healthy organs, symptoms, treatment, prognosis.
Through her stethoscope she listened to an infant's wheezing lungs.

No cure yet for pneumonia.
Her father so suddenly gone.

        She sips strong tea to ward off a cold

and thinks of the letter, the mess with Papa's business,
the mess with the insurance and he cannot set things straight.

Missing him squeezes her heart.
Study, Mama writes, *it's your job to study*.

She steadies her eyes on the page.

Late Night House Call

South Philadelphia

Lost, somewhere in blocks of rundown walk-ups
she ducks into Angelo's Bar and Grill,
stethoscope around her neck to protect her.

Dim stubbled faces look up—a woman alone—
someone recognizes the name on her paper,
someone else knows the address,
they send her fortified with directions
back to the neighborhood shrouded in rain

and she's looking for numbers on the buildings,
thinking of relatives back in Brooklyn,
what it will be like to climb three flights
knock on a strange family's door

and treat a woman she's never met,
twice her age, sick in bed,
who speaks no English and is in pain.

Dr. Kitty Mac

Expert on the female body's passages,
        how it drips, buds, empties, swells,

she deploys daily the arsenal of defense—
        biopsy, x-ray, radium, surgical technique,

but paramount, she urges, she insists:
        A good light and a suspicious mind,

perhaps half of early cases can be cured if caught in time.
        If caught in time.

Never married, she ministers to her brood,
        preparing them to heal, giving them the tools.

White-haired, wire-rimmed, dark suit and sturdy shoes,
        surgeon from her twenties as she'll be into her nineties,

she walks home to her mother
who pours her a cordial and asks about her day.

"Lady Killer"

What woman would agree to a pelvic exam
if she has no symptoms, no sign of disease,
can barely afford an ailing child's medicine
and never sees a doctor unless very sick—
blood, discharge, you-must-not-ignore-this,
go-to-the-hospital sick—
whose husband struggles to make the rent
and sees no reason to look for trouble
and whose doctor won't waste his time
on a healthy woman?

Senior Thesis: Preventable Carcinoma of the Uterine Cervix

> *Without guns, without uniforms, without poison gas, the Women's Field Army is mobilizing. The War on Cancer is a war we can win.* —Pamphlet of The American Society for the Control of Cancer

She stares at her title, so much to say,
the research behind her,
medical texts, clinical records,

the patients who answered her intimate questions.
But why did the cancer strike married women?

> Dr. Mac trained her. The pelvic exam.
> *Don't be timid, you need to know,*
> *right now we can save lives,*
> *the cure will come later.*

> Even what soothing words to use,
> *slight discomfort, bit of pressure.*

A doctor with a long Greek name
took vaginal smears from his own wife,
invented a test, nothing come of it yet,

meanwhile *the means exist*—

> An iodine swab, a colposcope,
> biopsy knife *even an intern could wield*—
> earnest words of the new recruit—

she rails against smug male physicians,
exhorts wives and mothers: *Insist on help, Lose no time,*
she types away, almost a doctor,

tops of letters cut off—can't tell *or* from *of*—
an easy exam, straightforward diagnosis
but if a woman waits too long she'll die.

Conditions

Miss Resnick has failed two classes—Medical Jurisprudence again
Miss Kehoe has pulled herself up—three conditions down to one
Miss Holcom has lifted herself out of danger

Professors and Dean meet in Committee.
Women, they know the odds

consider who flails, struggles,
falls behind or fails,
                                    between D and F
                    suspended

examine each student's Condition
the likelihood of remedy

Has she the stamina   Has not applied herself   Shows signs of mental strain
Seems distracted by some personal matter   May not be cut out for
Health remains uncertain   A small loan will be arranged

Married against advice, asks to withdraw, will we be open to her return?

painstaking pages
minutes typed on onionskin

the individual circumstance
the professional decision

watched, warned
            repeat the exam or the year
                        be allowed to advance

on condition she studies   harder   stays healthy   is up to the grind
is not needed too much at home   keeps her love life in its place
finds money for the term bill   devotes herself to work
          enough to persevere

a shame to lose her—
a second chance
even a third

Delivery

when the head crowns
        shrieks   mess
she must concentrate
a doctor stays   she stays
        in control

the baby slips like a fish
        into her hands

she holds him up   slaps his bottom
        to start the lungs   breathing   on their own
              baby's first cries

she holds back her tears
that rush with the mother's

        and takes a good look—
        a healthy boy

        She wipes him dry
gives him to the sobbing mother to kiss, hug, put to breast,
        and leaves them, exultant.

Anisette

Her eighth, a home birth.
Easier as she gets better
used to it she'll never
get used to it

> (every routine delivery is unique
> she's taught and she is learning
> contractions, contradictions
>
> a wanted child, a child
> not always wanted)

In this shabby cluttered kitchen
she'll remember forever—
Grazie, grazie mille, Dottore
the father overflowing with joy
as he pours her a shot of anisette.

Class of '37

Commencement.
       She is ready.   Proud.   Maybe scared.   Ready.

My mother stands with her classmates
       in the parting shot of ceremony—

if the picture had been taken

the missing photograph
       in a steady file
              class after class

Women profs   woman President   women doctors
       in labs, exam rooms, hospital hallways,
making Grand Rounds   wielding the knife.

The last women's medical school—
       It will not shut its doors.

Year with no picture. But I want evidence,
I want to see her
       poised on that threshold.

       Girls, they called themselves.
What begins as a challenge becomes their code

       young women who go before   who follow.

Photograph, the year after hers:
       new doctors grouped close
       three solid tiers

       not summer dresses of earlier pictures
         florals and prints—

they wear mortarboards, academic gowns
       that erase their separate shapes

place value on each beaming face

women she knew   colleagues, friends
          strangers to me

I want to know what she looked like
          that given day
                    what smile

Beneath her robe what dress did she wear?

After

Blackout Cake, World War II

What a sweet tooth Brooklyn had going for it—
every neighborhood, an Ebinger's down the block,
Avenue M, Flatbush, King's Highway,
cheese Danish, almond rings, mocha seven-layer—
My mother never indulged
too much at once,
how she kept her shape,
a piece when she earned it
or the prize she set her heart on
loomed out of reach.

Blackout. Midnight.
Three devil's food layers,
dark chocolate filling piled thick in-between,
chocolate pudding pillowing top and sides
covered by smothers of chocolate crumbs.
Way too rich to be good
for you, wasn't that the point?

During the War people slung black
across Brooklyn's windows
to blot the Navy Yard from enemy eyes,
hide transports launching toward Europe—
Loose lips sink ships!
It won't be good unless it's perfect—
be prepared for blackouts!
People lowered their car beams
or stationed themselves behind thick drapes
while the air drills wailed—

Bakeries got the precious sugar,
essential non-essential
to keep life on an even keel.
For something sweet that wasn't rationed
you went to Ebinger's—fresh-baked store-bought—
after all those years of Depression meals
and now your son or sweetheart overseas.

Honeymoon, Lake Minisinakwa, 1946

In a canoe never before
one like this   wild lake turning rough
picks up rhythm
she hadn't known of it
wilderness   romance
she can't swim he knows
these things   how to shift
weight to keep steady
growing turbulent
how to jack the paddle
keep the keel   on course
keep from tipping
she can't swim
water roiling ugly
whitecaps out of nowhere
what if
he tells her steady,
he's yelling at her
keep steady
he's doing his best against the swells
he's strong but he's
the gear the picnic lunch the prized camera
she panics she can't
swim
the canoe capsizes
she goes under she's gasping she's
he grabs her and
the canoe and
yes the paddle somehow
rights it
pulls her in she pulls herself
together
the camera's lost
despite his dives
she sees he regrets it
they reach shore
a good marriage begins

Sustenance

Mom taught us I Spy on the Indian Trail
behind our house, taught us to look for berries

though God forbid we put them in our mouths.
Doctor for the Brooklyn Board of Health,

she bought our tomatoes in cellophane,
washed and plunked hard chartreuse peaches

right in the crisper, to save us
from germs we couldn't see.

Dad, who had doctored in the Ontario Bush
straight from med school, through the Depression,

then had run a field hospital in Belgium
during the War, understood short rations

and would not in words gainsay her,
she brought him such taste and bounty.

X-Ray Machine

Mom and Dad for a special treat
give us a ride up and down
on the x-ray table. I climb aboard,

lie flat with my head on the pillow,
then the platform slowly tilts—
raises me upright, lowers me again,

but patients don't get to ride,
they must do as told, stand or lie,
allow the risk for their own good—

it's called *Exposure*—
they scramble onto the shiny black bed
whose metal arm comes close and cold,

then Mom takes the lead apron
from its hook and straps it on.
Heavier than a bathtub of water.

She steps behind the door
and presses the control,

we hear, through the storeroom wall
that separates the kitchen from the office,

Don't move   don't breathe   hold it—
        Relax.
Again,
        Take a deep breath   don't move
             hold it—   Relax.

Before-Dinner Drinks

He saw the husbands, she saw the wives,
so they could put two and two together.
Women chose her for a doctor more
like themselves—men went to him,
straightforward about what to do
beyond check-ups and vital signs.

My parents sat in twin living room chairs
under the lamp, sipping Canadian Club,
talking in low voices a mumbo-jumbo
of hemoglobin, blood count, EKG,
code more secret than Yiddish
as if they went on private rounds

each evening without us,
consulting about the day's revelations
of other men's and women's bodies
examined behind separate doors
in the office beneath their bedroom.

Until dinner, all of us at the table.

Internal Medicine

How a blouse hung from the shoulder, pleats fell from the hip,
seams cut on the bias. She kept her figure cinched,
wore a girdle and satin slip—the right foundations,

classic style with a bohemian touch,
houndstooth accented by silk batik,
navy swirled with fuchsia, fused with mint.

She dubbed the changing cubicle the Dressing Room.
A patient would strip to panties, put on a limp gown,
emerge to climb the examining table

so my mother could look, palpate, gently prod—
heartbeat and belly sounds, stethoscope, otoscope,
cuff and bulb, say *ah*, feet in stirrups for the g-y-n.

My patients notice what I wear she said
trying on frames at Trapp Opticians,
settling on tortoiseshell chased with gold—

not the commonplace cat's eyes with rhinestones—
bifocals for looking down at a chart,
then at the woman sitting by her desk

while she blended empathy with advice,
wrote a scrip on her prescription pad
and looking up, eye to eye, handed it
like a recipe across a kitchen table.

Autoclave

She'd say *Injection*. Never Shot. Shot was slang,
gave the wrong idea. She didn't say *Hurt*.
Just a *pinch* to keep you well or make you better.

She would stick the needle
in the upturned vial of vaccine,
hold the syringe above eye level
and pull back the plunger
to the measured line,
then plink her fingernail on the glass.
Squinch your eyes, she's done.

Dirty disassembled hypodermics—
needles, plungers, empty tubes—
idle and harmless in their limbo
waiting for the autoclave.

Keep back—hotter than the stove.
A pressure cooker, a breadbox,
a lobsterpot of high-gloss steel.

Later she unlocked its little door and with a forceps
lifted the sterilized parts to a laundered cloth.
It pleased me, the row of good-as-new hypodermics,

the autoclave like a big steaming heart,
rising to a boil then cooling to a sigh—
you could trust a needle after its trial by fire,
brought to the point of no return and back.

Developing X-Rays in the Basement Darkroom

Pungent smell of vinegar, ripe fruit.
Maybe this is what it's like to be dead,
seeing nothing.
The door has shut, we crowd in with our father,
eyes adjusting slowly to total dark,
then almost-dark lit by one red bulb.
We wait for his Dracula laugh,
deep, deliciously scary.
He has set the kitchen timer.
We don't move—
must not touch anything, jostle his work
or be splashed by chemicals as we feel him pivot
inches away, submerging films on metal frames
into the steel vats, lifting them from solution
when time is up.
He can read the secrets of strangers.
Around us forms emerge from negatives,
shadow tissue inside the darkroom of ribs.

Timepiece

Sweep-second hand, plain face
almost big as a man's,
my mother adds it last
after her make-up and tailored dress,
then descends from the sunny spread
of bedroom to the Office downstairs

where time becomes measurable.
She takes the vitals of her patients:
blood pressure with cuff, pumping bulb,
the slowly falling gauge,
temperature (three minutes until the tube
slides out from under the tongue),
pulse (ten seconds multiply by six).
Her eyes dart to her watch

and since women have worries
that may not fit time slots in the book
sometimes she runs over, gets backed up.

By afternoon she goes upstairs, changes
into sweater, slacks, low heels,
still wearing Lady Timex—
its daily nub for setting and winding.
I try it on, pretend I can tell time.
Time us, we say, how long it takes
to tie our laces, brush our teeth,
run around the house. *How many seconds?*
Did I win? We want that careful noticing,
the glance at her watch, the smile.

For parties she wears the Tissot
our father gave her, sign of his love
and their mutual journey,
a pearl dial with intricate numerals.
Then she lays her Timex on the dresser,
lifts the gold watch from its satin.
He works the delicate catch on her wrist.

Back Stairs

run up   run down   squeeze past,
down \   / up

I hear footsteps climbing behind a closed door
from the room past the kitchen

narrow, secondary—

(not like the front staircase
wide and carpeted
with banister, spindles, landing)—

this for single file

their bedroom right above the Office
quick getaway

back stairs for trays   tea, dry toast
Mom in bed   migraine
starting late

I hear footsteps
          descending—

to the kitchen, house, us?

or to the patients
(don't make them wait)?

back stairs for secrets,
narrow window at the bottom, a ledge
broad enough to hold a vase,

a child

could read there   hide things   hide

footsteps   hers, his
mounting /   \ descending

Steeplejack

Twice a year Dad and I climbed to the attic.
He'd take out his pocket knife,
pry open the midget door to the eaves,
point the torch into that dark
while I ducked through—

balancing on parallel joists—
sneaker toes, knees, heel of one hand,
tools clutched in the other—
planning each move,

squeezing—panic!—past the shaftway
that gaped three stories down. Once I dropped
his favorite screwdriver,

it fell to some resting place deep in the foundation.

The old mortar-and-lath—no solid floor,
just mica chips between the timbers. I played
my flashlight on water pipes,
stalactites of nails, glints of grinning mica—

I sidled out, wedged beneath roofline,
to open the vent in spring, close it in fall.

Private eye, poking for leaks and nests,
feeling for damp. Tufts, acorn shells, droppings
were warnings, whatever found its way inside
to dwell secretly with us, lead to damage.

Just as Mom and Dad studied x-rays for spots between ribs.

He called me his steeplejack, his barrelhouse monkey,
I fit into spaces he could not
while my mother and sisters and grandmother
stayed below in the sturdy, generous rooms.

Practice

makes perfect   motor memory   sleight of hand
    practice piano   ace the exam

life's not a dress rehearsal

    Keep practicing

tie your shoes   tie a bow   tie a suture with one hand

internship   residency   license to dispense

        license to practice in the State of New York

        You've got it
            You're almost there
                Keep up the good work

starting out   set up a practice   hang up a shingle   spread the word

    private practice   husband and wife

complete physical   vital signs   feet in the stirrups

firm hand   kind touch   gentle pressure
    —deep breath now cough

matter of trust   practice what you preach   write a scrip

    Keep practicing

common practice   up to date   practice makes perfect
    quit while you're ahead

beat the clock   glass half full   hourglass figure

    state of the art   aged to perfection

    still practicing

Home / Office

for Rita and Bill

Do you remember Mom or Dad dashing from office to kitchen
reaching in the fridge for the cardboard box
where they kept the vaccines,

how they used memo pads from drug companies
for grocery lists and phone numbers,

do you remember the lab box by the office door,
the milk-box on the back steps,

do you remember the magazines Mom subscribed to—
a few weeks on our coffee table before the waiting room:
National Geographic, Newsweek, New Yorker, Bazaar,

how Mom taught us to make hospital corners,
to scrub our hands like surgeons so we wouldn't get polio,
to be brave when we needed a shot,

do you remember her tea and burnt toast with cottage cheese,
getting ready for the office when we went off to school

then when we got back she'd be ready for us,
the snack she called *refreshments:* milk and Lorna Doones,

how when we stayed home sick she ran upstairs
between patients to see us, felt our foreheads,
in the afternoon read us poems, played gin rummy,

taught us never to pick up mercury with our fingers
if a thermometer broke, though it was fun to do?

How her name was Dr. Levin in the office,
Mrs. Susman for our teachers and for going out with Dad?

Do you remember *Never go to bed angry?*
Laugh and the world laughs with you, cry and you cry alone?
Don't leave the house without a kiss?

My Mother

I wish I'd told you.
                    Maybe I did,
or I forgot   or you've forgotten
I told you,

my voice now
          can only be
one you hear
               inside you
          once in a while, though

If I could stay with you,
sit with you, *tochtele,*

          I wouldn't need
to tell you,

you'd know
what I knew,

          day-to-days,
past pastimes
          names and places
to go with old photos,
               crumbling memories.

          You wouldn't need
to make me up

a story of the truth.

Meeting

I'm a day tripper in these woods,
once I find the trail it becomes the way back

no matter how often I've lost it.
My way. The trail. The past,

though my steps leave no imprint
heading towards you and where you've gone

to where I'm going—the trail grows shorter
and vivid pale beneath soft needles,

past and desire sifted together.
Sometimes you simply appear,

I haven't foreshadowed your mood,
your frame of mind, the clothes you wear,

even the year you return from—
while other times I summon you,

meet me on the trail,
conjuring the version of vision

you'll bring to me, just as once,
in no past either of us remembers,

I pushed from you, drawn forward
into the present world.

Notes on the Poems

Matriculation Book, September 14, 1933
Of the 33 women who signed the book that year, only 23 graduated four years later.

Accreditation
In 1935, when my mother was halfway through medical school, the College almost lost its accreditation, due largely to hidden gender bias against women in the profession and fear of competition for patients during the Depression years.

President Starr Reacts
Sarah Logan Wister Starr, born into the Philadelphia aristocracy, served as President of Woman's Med for twenty years and steered it through several crises.

Nicodemus
Nicodemus was the nickname given to the obstetrics practice doll. There were no Black students at Woman's Med in the 1930s.

Baby Clinic
The Barton Dispensary and Health Clinic in South Philadelphia, run by the College and staffed by its students, treated residents of a poor neighborhood who otherwise had little access to health care.

Dr. Kitty Mac
Catherine MacFarland, M.D., Professor of Obstetrics and Gynecology, was a pioneer in research and early screening for women's cancers. She taught generations of Woman's Med students, and won the prestigious Lasker Award for Clinical Medical Research.

Senior Thesis
In keeping with the mission of Woman's Med, graduating students were required to write a senior thesis on a topic in preventive medicine.

Delivery
To graduate and receive her prized white coat, a student had to deliver ten babies.

Sources

These research sources were extremely helpful:

Legacy Center Archives and Special Collections, Drexel University College of Medicine, Philadelphia.

Minutes of the Proceedings of the Forty-Sixth Annual Meeting, Association of American Medical Colleges, Toronto, Canada, October 28, 29, and 30, 1935. (www.aamc.org/about/history/foundations).

A New and Untried Course: Woman's Medical College of Pennsylvania, 1850-1998 by Steven J. Peitzman (Alumnae and Alumni Assn. of MCP Hahnemann School of Medicine, 2000).

Sympathy and Science: Women Physicians in American Medicine by Regina Morantz-Sanchez (U. of North Carolina Press, 2000).

Transactions of the Alumnae Association, Woman's Medical College of Pennsylvania, 1935.

Acknowledgments

I am grateful to smart, generous friends and readers who responded with helpful feedback and encouragement through drafts of these poems: my critique and performance group The Cool Women Poets, my dear Four Friends Poets group, US 1 Poets Cooperative, and my students at the Osher Lifelong Learning Institute at Rutgers University. Thanks to Mark Doty whose classes I audited at Rutgers, and to Martha Collins, Joan Wickersham, and Robin Coste-Lewis at the Fine Arts Work Center, Provincetown, MA, who guided me in writing poetry about history. My gratitude to Coleen Marks for her excellent help with the photos, and to archivist Matt Herbison at Drexel University.

Thanks especially to my first and best readers, my husband Jay Harris and my sister Rita Wolpert; my children Owen and Suzanne; and deepest thanks to my parents Carol and Ben Susman, who gave me their love and their stories.

The following poems appeared first in these journals:

"After / Before" and "Pneumonia" in *Drexel University College of Medicine Alumni Magazine*.
"Back Stairs" in *The Westchester Review*.
"Before Dinner Drinks" in a different form, and "Late Night House Call," in *View from the Bed View from the Bedside* (Wising Up Press).
"Developing X-Rays in the Basement Darkroom," in *US1 Worksheets* and *Gogama* (Sheltering Pines Press).
"For My Grandmother" in *US1 Worksheets*.
"Honeymoon, Lake Minisinakwa," in *Slant*.
"Internal Medicine" in different form in *CHEST, Journal of the American College of Chest Physicians*.
"Steeplejack" in *Poet Lore*.
"Sustenance" in *Familiar* (Finishing Line Press).

About the Author

Maxine Susman has published six previous poetry collections, and her poems appear widely in journals and anthologies. After a career as Professor of English at Caldwell University, she now teaches poetry writing and fiction at the Osher Lifelong Learning Institute of Rutgers University, where she earned the Distinguished Teaching Award. Born in New York City, she grew up in Westchester County, lives in New Jersey, and goes walking in the Catskills, Cape Cod, and Maine. She writes about nature and the environment, art, personal history, and shifting states of body and mind: *My Mother's Medicine* follows books set in Northern Ontario, on outer Cape Cod, and in Paris during World War II.

CPSIA information can be obtained
at www.ICGtesting.com
Printed in the USA
FFHW021114180719
53692476-59400FF